Circ
Sca

Written by Alison Milford
Illustrated by Enzo Troiano

FULL FLIGHT

Titles in Full Flight Fear & Fun

Space Plague
Bubble Attack
Circus Scam
Evil Brain Chips
Football Killers
Skyrunners
Spook Manor
Dark Detective
Valley of Wisdom
Maxi Beasts

Badger Publishing Limited
Oldmedow Road, Hardwick Industrial Estate,
King's Lynn PE30 4JJ
Telephone: 01438 791037

www.badgerlearning.co.uk

2 4 6 8 10 9 7 5 3 1

Circus Scam ISBN 978 1 84691 126 2

First edition © 2007
This second edition © 2013

Series Editor: Jonny Zucker
Publisher: David Jamieson
Commissioning Editor: Carrie Lewis
Editor: Paul Martin
Design: Fiona Grant
Illustration: Enzo Troiano (Beehive Illustration)

Circus Scam

Contents

1. The circus is here! 4

2. Circus parade secret 8

3. First night disaster! 10

4. A button and a box 14

5. Terror in the ring! 18

6. Catch that clown! 24

7. Circus surprises! 28

Badger LEARNING

1. The circus is here!

The All Stars Circus had come to Crosston for the summer holidays. Amazing acrobats, funny clowns, clever jugglers and fearless trapeze artists got ready as the Big Top was pulled up into place.

What's his problem, Bill?
I've turned down his offer of a large sum of money to take the circus out of town.

Why would he want to do that?
Because he owns the local funfair…
…and we'll be taking away his customers.

He won't be happy when he hears about Anya, the new star of our show.

But *I'm* the star of this circus. Everyone loves Marco the Clown!
Want to bet?!
THEGRU
CIR

Lena! Stop juggling and get my parade costume ready, now!
Yes, sir!
THEGRU

2. Circus parade secret

Later that afternoon, the circus paraded through the town.

But not everyone was happy.

From out of the shadows, a voice answered back.

3. First night disaster!

That evening…

But up in the back of the tent…

Something's wrong with Dani!
I can't see!

Arghh! I'm falling!

Are you all right, Dani?
I've hurt my leg!

That light seemed to be coming from the back of the tent.
Look! Somebody's up there!

But at the back of the tent...

4. A button and a box

Next morning...

We think someone may have wanted to make Dani fall.
Ha! Dani fell because she's hopeless at balancing!

Box for Marco the Clown.
Good! Just what I've been waiting for.

Zoe and Jake secretly followed Marco to his caravan.

Lena!
What are you two doing here?
We think Marco is planning to ruin the show tonight!

We'd better go and warn Bill.
No, I'll do it.

5. Terror in the ring!

A few hours later…

Should the water cannon be pointing that way?
No! Marco! Not there!

Suddenly…

Argh!
Splutter!
Cough!

As the cloud of dust goes down...

But outside, Marco had vanished.

Jake and Zoe rushed to the ring to stop Anya from starting her performance.

Help! Get the safety net!

Thank goodness! Anya's safe!

6. Catch that clown!

Suddenly…

Get out of my way, you idiot!
Hey! That's my bike. Come back!

Oh, no! He's getting away.
Quick! Throw these balls in front of him.

We know you're working for the funfair boss.
Give yourself up, Marco!
Never!

Perhaps this will change your mind!
Arggh!

With one lasso of the rope...
... Marco the Clown is tied up ready for the police.

Wonderful!
CLAP!
CLAP!
CLAP!
Amazing!
Bravo!

7. Circus surprises!

A few minutes later, backstage…

But you nearly killed Anya and destroyed our circus!
And I would have got away with it if it wasn't for you sticking your noses in.

But why are you in Marco's costume?
Because I wanted that nasty old clown to take all the blame.

We've picked up the funfair owner.
I guess he and Lena will be going to prison for quite some time.
POLICE

Lena was very good at being Marco, wasn't she?
But where is the real Marco?

Inside Marco's caravan...

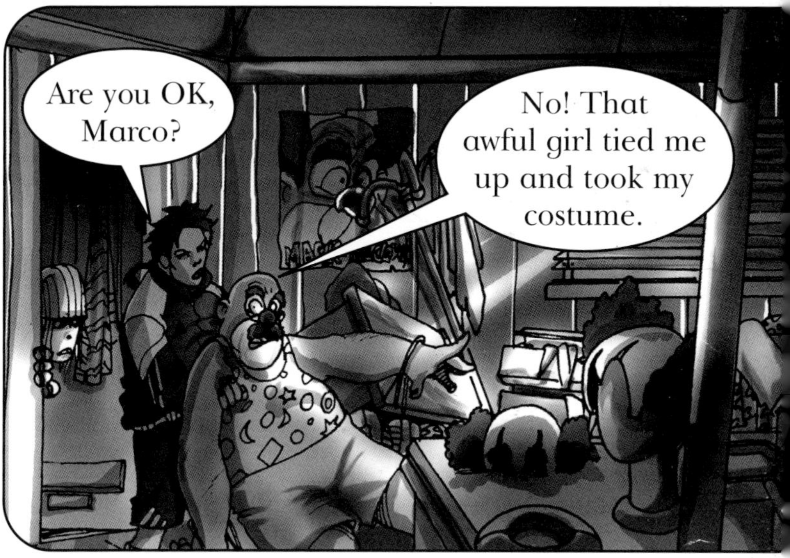

An ultra powerful flower water pistol!
MAIL
Ha! Ha!
Stop laughing! Everyone's gone mad! I'm the only sane person here.